Don't buy your **kitchen chimney** without reading this!

The Ultimate Kitchen Chimney Survival Guide

Don't buy your **kitchen chimney** without reading this!

The Ultimate Kitchen Chimney Survival Guide

GURJOT SINGH GULATI

Worldwide Published by
Pendown Press

PENDOWN PRESS

An ISO 9001 & ISO 14001 Certified Co.,
Regd. Office: 2525/193, 1st Floor, Onkar Nagar-A,
Tri Nagar, Delhi-110035
Ph.: 09350849407, 09312235086
E-mail: info@pendownpress.com
Branch Office: 1A/2A, 20, Hari Sadan, Ansari Road,
Daryaganj, New Delhi-110002
Ph.: 011-45794768
Website: PendownPress.com

First Edition: 2022

ISBN: 978-93-91544-68-3

Layout and Cover Designed by Pendown Graphics Team
Printed and Bound in India by Thomson Press India Ltd.

Dedication

I lovingly dedicate this book to my parents, my sister, my son Gurvansh, my wife Simer and my mentors, who have been my constant support system.

Praises

Here is more awesome feedback from those who have benefited from Gurjot's expert guidance.

Kitchen Chimney market is over crowded with options. One is bound to get confused and choose wrong product. But I was fortunate to attend Gurjot Singh's Masterclass on How to select right chimney for your Kitchen. With Gurjot's smart advice I was able to buy exact-fit for our kitchen. Thank you Gurjot!

–Payal Yadav
Proud Homemaker & Entrepreneur

Before meeting Gurjot, we never knew selecting a kitchen chimney required such in-depth analysis. He explains every feature in depth, understand client needs & filters out the best suitable product for them. I'm now satisfied that my clients have spent their hard-earned money on this modern gadget wisely. Thank you, Gurjot.

–Harshita Goel & Zeenat Afreen
Urban Indoors, Interior Designers

When Gurjot approached me for a meeting to give a presentation on his products, I thought it would be just another presentation like others have always been presenting.

I have come across many presentations in my career, but the presentation he gave was unique and something that I have never seen in my career. He believes in adding value to my work & and providing knowledge to my clients.

–Sujata Poddar
3 Corner Designs, Interior Designer

Gurjot prevented my client from wasting Rs.1,10,000/- through his timely advice on chimneys.

–Ayindrilla & Arkadeepa Bhattacharya
Spacebox Interiors, Interior Designer

It was after attending Gurjot's presentation on chimneys that I realized that I had wasted huge amounts of money by blindly trusting the vendors who were either inexperienced or simply interested in selling their merchandise. I really wish I had access to this knowledge on chimneys before selecting a chimney for my Kitchen.

–Krunal Garach

Khodal Kraft Interiors, Interior Designer

It gives me utmost pleasure to thank Mr. Gurjot Singh Gulati for an exceptionally prompt response and an expeditious service ethic.

I feel he has the one stop solution to all my chimney, Hobs and other kitchen requirements.

In every deal he has personally taken out time to understand the complex requirements of my clients and have created a personalized service plan that helped streamline the processes.

We really appreciate the time he and his team of experts have dedicated and putting an end to our search hassles of cooking solutions.

–Dhiraj Bhansaly

Architect, Ambiance designs

All households are in constant need of some, or the other appliances. This is where I met Mr. Gurjot Singh Gulati from Eastern Agencies. It started with taking quotes from him & comparing them with market rates. Rates can always be matched, but what they stand out at is their impeccable guidance & service.

I was looking for a kitchen chimney. Mr. Gurjot himself took the initiative to explain to me why we need the same and which model would suit our needs–even without me asking for it. I was impressed with his expertise in Chimney & Hobs & since then all appliances are bought from him without comparing rates.

I would highly recommend Gurjot & his team, for your home appliances needs. I wish him all the best for continued success!

–Sweta Agarwal

Ideal Insurance Brokers (P) Ltd.

Contents

Acknowledgements

This book would not have been possible without the help of many people, including my friends, family members and mentors.

I must credit my family first & foremost; without their support, this would not have been possible. My Father, Harvinder Singh Gulati, who built the base of the business & then trusted me to take it to newer heights. My mother, Satpal Kaur Gulati, who has always been a moral support to me & has ensured that I accomplish all my goals. My sister Nikita Gulati who has always supported me, my son Gurvansh Singh Gulati who has given me a reason to smile & stay happy.

I would like to express sincere gratitude to my mentors and guides Mr. Dibyendu Das, Mrs. Purvee Mehrotra and Mr. Akshar Yadav for their unstinting guidance, support and motivation.

Last but not least, I would like to thank my wonderful wife, Simerpreet Gulati, for her continuous support and encouragement. This book and this journey would not have been possible without you – I love you...

Chapter 1

An Introduction–Why Your Kitchen Chimney may be the Most Important Kitchen Gadget in Your Home?

Do your eyes and nose often water when cooking due to the fumes arising from the pans and other cooking utensils? Do your family members rub their eyes in pain and rush outside when some spicy food is cooked in your Kitchen? Your answer depends on whether you have a quality kitchen chimney installed over your gas stove or not.

Chimneys have been part and parcel of domestic life in India and worldwide since time immemorial. Mostly, it is a chimney installed over the fireplace that enjoys all the limelight in movies and T.V. series. The kitchen chimney doesn't get much attention. Even during your favorite cooking reality shows, there is a great chance that you have never noticed the kitchen chimney, even if it is there.

Well, the chimneys have been ubiquitous. In rural households, since lots of coal and wood are used when cooking, almost every Kitchen has a chimney so that the toxic fumes can escape without choking the people sitting in the Kitchen. Despite that, before the advent of gas-based cooking, hundreds of thousands of people suffered from lung ailments because they constantly inhaled the toxic fumes coming out of their earthen ovens.

In urban households, just because you're using an expensive oven and a gas connection doesn't mean that you are not exposed to harmful fumes and chemicals when cooking.

There are toxic pollutants in your Kitchen. There is even carbon monoxide when you're cooking. In the absence of a good chimney, humid and oily deposits begin to settle around the cooking area giving rise to bacteria and germs. When you install a good-quality chimney, all the fumes, gases, and toxic pollutants are sucked out and released into the outer air. The humidity and the oily gases are constantly being sucked by your Chimney, leaving your Kitchen cool and clean.

What I'm saying is, a good quality chimney is essential to the good health of your Kitchen.

Why am I giving you so much expert advice on chimneys?

Hello, my name is Gurjot Singh Gulati, and I am in the business of selling Electrical Home Appliances. My father started his appliances business, Eastern Agencies, back in 1986, and after completing my education, I joined my family business. Ever since, I have had a great time making new contacts, building lasting relationships, growing the business, and extending a helping hand to our customers whenever there is a need or an opportunity.

Overall these years, I have successfully helped mothers and homemakers who love cooking for their families get rid of smoke and odor in their kitchens. How was it made possible? By installing the marvelously modern kitchen gadget called the "kitchen chimney."

The journey so far has been extremely satisfying and enchanting.

However, seeing so many people not truly understanding the need for a chimney and then battling with finding the right Chimney with very little guidance and information available in the market. I felt compelled to share my knowledge with everyone so that there is no home without a chimney and that every home has the most suitable Chimney. I haven't held myself back at all and have shared my expertise thoroughly in this book.

Here are a few testimonials that will help the readers understand the importance of a chimney:

Mr. Gurjot Singh Gulati helped me shortlist the kind of kitchen chimney needed for an ongoing site in Ahmedabad. Through his consultation, I saved money and time for my client, and in the process, I also gained lots of knowledge about kitchen chimneys.

I vouch for Mr. Gurjot Singh Gulati and have complete trust in his expert advice on selecting chimneys that lead to the finest kitchen design. I'm going to continue taking his expert consultation for all my future endeavors to make my clients' kitchens the best place in the house.

Apeksha Nagia
Interior Designer & Author

I have an open kitchen. The smoke and smell would often spread into my dining room, and sitting there would become difficult for my family members and guests.

Gurjot's proper guidance and technical expertise helped me create a "HEALTHY COOKING ENVIRONMENT." The Chimney extracts all the smoke, odor, and harmful gases that are produced during cooking.

Anju Saini
Alternate Healing Center

So, why this book?

There are multiple reasons:

1. Installing the right kitchen chimney is critical for your health. You spend a good amount of time in your Kitchen.
2. In India's humid and hot conditions, it can be torturous sometimes (assuming there is no A.C. in the Kitchen). Making food for your family should be an enjoyable experience. Even if you don't directly cook the food, the fumes that arise from your oven and the spices can make your family members sneeze, cough, and rub their eyes. It can be an everyday affair if there is no sufficient ventilation in your Kitchen.
3. With the information present in this book, you will be able to select just the right kitchen chimney for your Kitchen. This is one reason.
4. Another reason is that people are constantly approaching me for insights into kitchen chimneys and their various parts. I have been a distributor of Chimney Hoods for many years, and I have learned a lot about kitchen chimneys. All the information and knowledge that I have gained, I have gained working in the trenches. I have shared feelings of joy, and sometimes, even pain, with people who installed chimneys in their kitchens.
5. What's the best for me to buy? What all to keep in mind before investing in a good chimney? After all, you don't install a chimney often. Once you have installed it, you may be stuck with it for years to come.

6. It is not humanly possible to provide answers to all the good people. Making my book available is an easier, and to be frank, a much more efficient option. You can download the book on your mobile phone or laptop, and then you can go through it at your own pace. There is no rush. You can even save it as a Kindle book and then read it on your Kindle reader, lying luxuriously under a tree outside.
7. Often, when having one-on-one conversations, it is not possible to provide all the information. In this book, I can strategically organize everything and convey it in an understandable manner. And the great thing is, you can refer to the book whenever there is a need.

So, here I am, your friendly Chimney Hoods Expert, Gurjot Singh Gulati.

Chapter 2

What is a Kitchen Chimney? What are its Dynamics?

In this e-book, I have often referred to the kitchen chimney as a "Modern Gadget." Why call it a modern gadget?

Kitchen chimneys today are not your traditional chimneys that simply allow the smoke and the fumes to escape through the roof of your house. They use modern suction techniques. An elaborate exhaust system is embedded within the modern-day kitchen chimney that sucks smoke and fumes even from the surrounding areas.

Until a few years ago, most of the households didn't even have chimneys. If they were slightly aware or were extra sensitive to the fumes, they would install an exhaust fan near the roof.

Since people inside the Kitchen, primarily mothers and homemakers, got used to toxic fumes, smells, grease, and smoke, in many unfortunate cases, even began to succumb to the constant onslaught without knowing the concept of installing modern-day kitchen chimneys wasn't taken seriously.

Nowadays, most kitchen installations consist of an electric chimney too. Since it's an electric chimney and proactively sucks out smoke and fumes, we can easily call it a modern gadget.

Working in a kitchen without a chimney can be hazardous, especially when you do it every day.

A kitchen seems friendly, no? Most of your nourishment comes from your Kitchen. A big part of your childhood memories consists of food prepared by your mother. When you grow up and get married, either you cook, or your spouse does. In any case, cooking food is an integral part of growing up and living your life. The day begins with something being cooked, and it also ends with something being cooked.

Remember those old movies when they showed a woman blowing into an earthen oven with an iron pipe and coughing in the process? It was either a tearjerker scene of someone being mistreated or a romantic scene showing the female protagonist taking care of her family. Very few paid attention to the coughing part.

When the government launched the Pradhan Mantri Ujjwala Yojana to distribute more than 50 million cylinders in rural India, especially for families below the poverty line, it wasn't just a political move. Traditional kitchen smoke is one of the biggest killers in rural India. This smoke mostly comes from burning wood, coal, dung, and other random inflammable materials the villagers can easily burn.

In rural kitchens, the occupants are exposed to pollutants like particulates, carbon monoxide, nitrogen oxide, benzene, formaldehyde, 1,3-butadiene, and other polyaromatic compounds. Over 800 million people in India are affected by the smoke and fumes generated in the Kitchen. 1 million people die annually due to kitchen pollution, according to the Lancet Respiratory Medicine Commission.

We also need to keep in mind that it's not just women who spend time in these regions. When the kids are small, they stay with their mothers. Even when the mothers are pregnant, these fumes are causing health problems for them.

What about urban kitchens? They all have gas cylinders or gas pipeline connections. Are they hazardous too?

Not everyone gets to live in a sprawling neighborhood where there are open spaces. In multistoried apartments and even in congested areas, no matter how luxurious your interiors are, your Kitchen can be highly hazardous if there is no proper ventilation or a kitchen chimney installed.

Although the gas inside your cylinder or the gas pipeline is constantly being burned, there is a residue that is continuously being released into the air. For example, carbon monoxide is odorless and tasteless, but it fills up your surroundings when you are using your gas stove. During frying and cooking, you heat the oil, fat, and other food ingredients, releasing unhealthy pollutants that can cause breathing problems.

If you're constantly feeling throat irritation, headaches, fatigue, and nausea, your Kitchen definitely needs a chimney. Children and youngsters with asthma can be particularly troubled in the vicinity of the Kitchen.

Fumes in a typical kitchen may consist of nitrogen dioxide, carbon monoxide, carbon dioxide, volatile organic compounds, and even carcinogens.

A kitchen chimney is a must for every Kitchen. You should preferably get a duct able chimney. As the name suggests, this Chimney has a duct (a metallic tunnel) that extends outside through the wall or the window. It sucks all the pollutants and fumes from your Kitchen and throws them out.

The other option does not have a duct. It sucks in the smoke and the pollutants and runs them through a filter and then, from the top, releases the clean air back into your Kitchen. It may not be very effective, and you may have to routinely clear the filter for your Chimney for it to work efficiently.

What are the general oversights committed by customers when buying a chimney for the Kitchen?

Frankly, I wouldn't call them oversights because, well, you don't buy a chimney repeatedly. For most of you, it may be the first time you are planning on installing a chimney in your Kitchen. You may have done it a couple of times, but this doesn't give you enough experience to make the right decision. Here are a few mistakes people commit:

- **What's the purpose?** Yes, they are installing a chimney, but they may be installing it just because the others do it. They don't know why they are installing it, and since they don't know, they fail to choose the right Chimney for the right purpose.
- **Complete trust in the vendor:** Remember the vendor is just interested in selling you the Chimney, least bothered by what your requirement is. The same is with the contractor responsible for refurbishing your Kitchen. They are going to install a piece that is best for them, not for you. Hence, it is imperative to weigh in and ensure that you get an appropriate chimney for your Kitchen.
- **Leaving it on the salesperson:** When they visit a store, they leave it to the salesperson to decide what type of Chimney they should have for the Kitchen.

- **Going for the low-priced Chimney:** A low-priced chimney comes with weaker motor power. Please remember that you want your Chimney to suck in as many fumes, gases, and smoke varieties as possible. Not just underneath the Chimney but also from the surrounding areas.
- **Just for the heck of it:** Many people install chimneys because they look good in the Kitchen. They think it is like a showpiece that modern kitchens must have or because their neighbors have it installed in their kitchens.
- **No research:** They don't spend much time researching and trying to know which would be the best chimney installation for the Kitchen.
- **Not considering the cooktop/hob size:** Your kitchen chimney must cover an area wider than your Cooktop or your hob; otherwise, much of the fumes will be escaping from the sides. Although the suction power of the Chimney should be able to suck in gases and fumes even from the surrounding areas, it is best to get a wider chimney than the cooking area.
- **Selection after Renovation:** Waiting for the renovation to be finished before choosing your Cooktop and Chimney. This may not leave you with enough space to accommodate the size of the Cooktop you desire.
- **More focus on looks:** There are many kitchen chimneys with much show & pomp and no performance. Customers get swayed by the design and the look of the Chimney rather than focusing on the quality of the motor and the suction power.

Chapter 3

What Factors or Features should You Consider when Buying a Kitchen Chimney Explained with the Help of a Story

Once a customer visited my shop to buy a hob for his Kitchen. I suggested that he should also purchase a chimney.

He responded quite negatively, ***"Bekar hai, ye sab chimney kaam nahi karti."*** It is useless to install a kitchen chimney. They solve no purpose.

I asked him which Chimney he used and from where he got it.

He said that when he renovated his Kitchen and got modular kitchen work done, he had asked his contractor to install a chimney too. Beyond that, he knew nothing of the Chimney. All he knew was, a chimney doesn't solve any purpose, and it was mainly installed to give a modern look to the Kitchen.

While he was sharing his experience with me, his wife purchased the built-in hob from the cash counter.

I asked the couple if they looked into the factors that would have helped them purchase the right Chimney for their Kitchen. They both gave me a surprised look.

It wasn't surprising. Having sold kitchen gadgets, including chimneys, for years, I have encountered customers who have no clue about chimneys. I asked the following questions to them:

1. Did you measure the size of your Cooktop or hob and then choose the Chimney accordingly?
2. Did you measure the length of the duct pipe that is supposed to throw the kitchen fumes and smoke out?
3. Do you know there are multiple types of chimneys available in the market, including the flat Chimney, the hooded Chimney, and the Island chimney?
4. Do you know what type of filters are used in a chimney and how often a chimney requires maintenance?
5. Do you know the height of the Chimney directly impacts the amount of smoke, odor, and harmful gases that it can suck out?

   The couple gave me a blank look. They had no idea so much was to be considered before purchasing a kitchen chimney.

   The wife quietly asked me, "how many types of chimneys are there and what are the factors that must be considered before buying a kitchen chimney?"

I gave them a complete rundown on the various types of chimneys and how one should select the right Chimney according to one's kitchen setup. For elaboration and your benefit, I'm listing this information here.

Broadly, you must consider the following factors before you purchase a chimney for your Kitchen:

i. Chimney type

ii. Chimney filter types

iii. Chimney suction power (case study included)

iv. Chimney ducting

v. Chimney motor (case study included)

vi. Chimney size

Chimney Type

There are three types of kitchen chimneys, namely:

1. Wall-mounted Chimney
2. Island Chimney
3. Split Chimney

Which type of Chimney you choose depends on your kitchen structure, the amount of space you have, and the location of your cooking platform, hob, or stove.

The Wall-Mounted Chimney is fitted against the wall. Just make sure that the Cooktop or the hob is also located adjacent to the wall so that the Chimney covers the cooking area. A wall-mounted chimney can be either a flat chimney or a hooded chimney.

An island chimney is needed when your cooking area is located at the center of the Kitchen, that is, away from the wall.

The island chimney needs to hang from the roof or the ceiling of your Kitchen, precisely above the Cooktop or the hob.

Like the split A.C., the Split Chimney has two parts: one outdoor and one indoor unit. This is when you don't want extra sound in the Kitchen. All the machinery and the suction unit is outside. The part that captures the smoke and the fumes is naturally inside, above the Cooktop or the hob.

Types of Kitchen Chimney Filter

1. **Cassette/mesh filter**

2. **Baffle filter**

3. **Carbon filter**

Just as is the case with the type of Chimney, what filter you use depends on your kitchen conditions.

In cassette/mesh filters, there are multiple layers of aluminum or stainless steel mesh filters stacked together. This filter traps solid particles and allows the smoke to escape. As grease and oil particles deposit on the mesh filter and clog the spaces, it begins to affect the suction capabilities of the Chimney. These are high-maintenance filters. For better performance, they need to be washed every week.

Most of the Indian kitchen chimneys have a baffle filter. It is, in fact, better than the aluminum cassette/mesh filter, almost 30% better, according to the research. The panels on the filter have multiple curves that capture grease and oil while allowing the smoke to escape.

One annoying problem with these filters is that the particles get accumulated in the curves of the baffle filter. Then sometimes, these particles drip into what you're cooking, which can be unhealthy. Very easy to maintain. You can clean them once a month to avoid dripping. You don't need a technician to detach the filters and clean them.

Carbon filters are made of black charcoal, and hence, sometimes they are also called charcoal filters. These filters are mainly used for absorbing odor. If there is no duct in your Chimney, the carbon filter is used in combination with the baffle filter or the cassette filter. The oil, smoke, and grease particles get clogged inside the carbon filter, affecting your Chimney's performance. They need to be replaced every six months depending on the intensity of your cooking.

Chimney Suction Power

Suction power is the ability of your Chimney to suck smoke, oil particles, and smell from on top of the cooking area and the surrounding area.

For your kitchen chimney to work effectively, the suction power must be considered carefully and how much power it has, depends on the size of your Kitchen. The rule of thumb is that whatever your Kitchen's size, the Chimney has to fill 10x the air per hour. What does that mean?

Suppose your kitchen size is 4m × 4m × 2.5m = 40m^3. Your Chimney needs to fill 10 times your kitchen volume in an hour, which means 10 × 40m^3 = 400m^3 per hour. This is the suction power of your Chimney that you need: 400m^3.

Aside from the size, what sort of cooking you indulge in also must be factored in. Non-vegetarian food produces more smoke and smell compared to vegetarian food. Hence, when you cook non-vegetarian food, more suction power is needed.

If all this seems overwhelming, while buying your kitchen chimney, keep a roundabout figure of 700m^3/h to 1400m^3/h suction power when buying the Chimney.

Chimney Ducting

The duct of your Chimney is that squarish or a roundish tunnel or the passageway that throws your kitchen smoke, fumes, and smells out.

The performance of your Chimney depends on:

1. The size of the duct: the length and the diameter.
2. The number of bends in the duct.
3. Ideally, the length should be as small as possible, and the width must be at least 6 inches wide. Of course, the

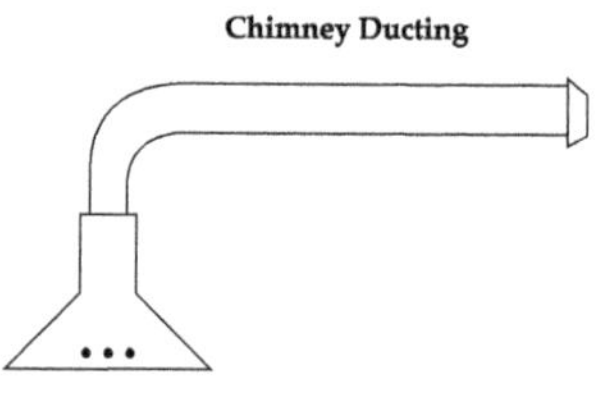

length depends on where your cooking area is located. The more the duct needs to travel to reach the outer wall of the Kitchen, the lengthier it will need to be.

4. Also, if the duct is not wide enough, it won't be able to suck in enough smoke and fumes.
5. The number of bends in the duct pipe before it reaches outside also affects the flow of the smoke. The greater the number of bends, the more suction power your Chimney needs to push the smoke and other stuff out.

The Motor or the Blower

This is the heart and soul of your Chimney. How efficiently your Chimney works, for how long it works, and how much power it consumes majorly depends on the motor of your Chimney.

Choose a motor that comes with a thermal overload protector. In the Kitchen, the motor can get overheated. When this happens, the motor with a thermal overload protector automatically cuts off power. This protects your motor from burning out and increases its life.

Go for a BLDC motor. BLDC stands for "brushless direct current." BLDC motors come with lots of benefits. They produce low heat. They create less noise. They increase or decrease RPM (rotations per minute) according to the amount of suction needed. If there is a blockage or extra smoke, the motor increases the RPM to put more power, and when things are normal, it reduces the RPM. Hence, it is an energy-efficient motor. It has been observed that compared to other motors, BLDC motors consume 40–50% less power.

The Chimney Size

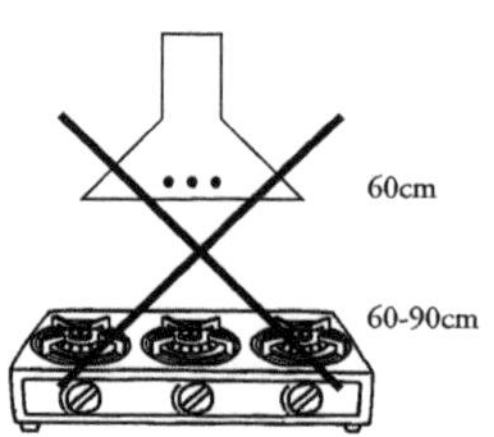

Finally, we come to the size. Always buy a chimney that is wider than the size of your cooking area or your hob. Never opt for a chimney that is smaller than your cooking area because this may result in a loss of efficiency.

What is the ideal size? If your Kitchen has 2/3/4 burner cooktop/hobs, then a 60cm or 75 cm width chimney is fine, but then make sure that the width of the cooktop/hob is also around 60 cm to 75 cm. If you have 3/4/5 burner cooktop/hobs of width 60-75 cm, then go with a 75/90cm width chimney. If you have 3/4/5 burner cooktop/hobs with a 75-90 cm width, then opt for a chimney with a width of 90 cm.

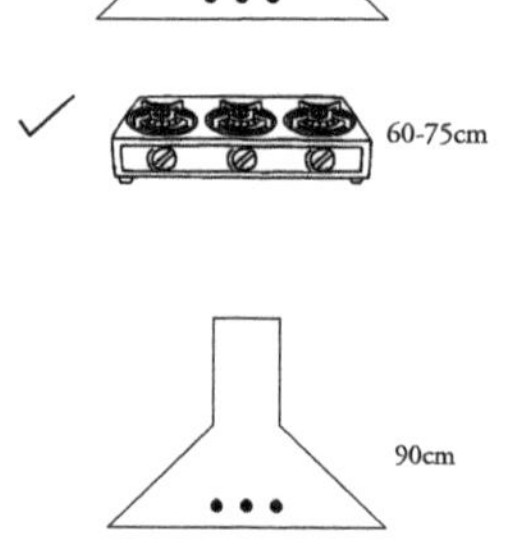

For your Chimney to work effectively, ensure that it is installed precisely above the cooking area and it is at least a few inches wider than the cooking area so that the smoke, gases, and fumes don't escape and pollute the Kitchen.

Maintenance & Cleaning

A kitchen chimney should suck in oil, greasy gases, cooking residue, and smell, filter the air, and then pump fresh air back into the Kitchen. In the process, the filter, the motor, and the other internal parts of the Chimney begin to get clogged. Regular maintenance is needed to open up the passageways, clear the filters, and keep the Chimney running.

There is also an unhygienic aspect of not cleaning the Chimney regularly. The accumulated oil deposited on the filter begins to drip into the food being cooked after a while.

There is also a health hazard. The oil that gets deposited inside the Chimney is inflammable. With heat and exposure to a spark, it can ignite and cause a fire.

Hence, it is recommended that:

- The filter of the Chimney is cleaned at regular intervals. Preferably, the mesh/cassette filter should be cleaned once a week and the baffle filters once a fortnight.
- The inner body and the motor of the Chimney should be cleaned by a technician from an authorized service center at least twice a year.

How to Clean the Filter?

The process of cleaning your chimney filter can be time-consuming or not, depending on whether you're using a mesh filter or a baffle filter. As mentioned above, a baffle filter requires less maintenance than a mesh filter.

Household cleaners can be used to clean your filter. You can use dish washing liquid, baking soda, paint thinner or caustic soda to prepare your cleaning concoction.

Anyway, here is the process of cleaning your chimney filter:

- Fill a tub with hot water. Make sure the tub is big enough to submerge the chimney filter sufficiently.
- Add some dishwater liquid soap, or sprinkle baking soda or caustic soda on the filter.
- Immerse the filter in hot water.
- Let it soak for an hour or more.
- Take it out and brush or scrub it.

- You can repeat the process if you feel the filter needs more cleaning.
- Rinse the filter in clean water and leave it under the sun to dry.
- Put it back into the Chimney.

Can you get a chimney in which you can avoid the hassle of cleaning the filters often?

Are there chimneys available that clean themselves? Yes, you can buy a chimney that cleans itself. An auto-clean button on the Chimney activates a heating system inside the Chimney to melt the accumulated oil and grease. This melted oil and grease is collected in a cup or a tray. You can take out the cup or the tray, clean it, and then put it back into the Chimney.

Are Auto-cleaning Chimneys Better?

They definitely require less maintenance. The accumulated oil and grease can be a big nuisance, and if the auto-cleaning system can get rid of them, a lot of strain is not put on the motor, and the life span of your chimney increases.

Recap

Here's a quick recap of what I have covered in the book. It is in the form of questions and answers and hence, easier to grasp.

Do you need a chimney?

The short answer is yes, the long answer is if you feel there are gases and fumes and greasy smoke in your Kitchen that can make the person (mostly your housemaker–your wife or your mother) working in the Kitchen extremely uncomfortable and sick over a period of time, then a definitive yes.

Please remember that the smoke that comes from your Kitchen is a silent killer. It may not show any adverse signs, and then suddenly, the person may get extremely sick.

What chimney design should I use?

The design of the Chimney depends on the make of your Kitchen. If there is sufficient height available, then go with a hood chimney. Otherwise, go for a flat chimney. Go with a wall-mounted chimney if your cooking area or the hob is near the wall. Otherwise, you can get an island chimney.

Which filter should I opt for?

There are three choices: mesh/cassette filter, baffle filter, or charcoal filter. All the filters have their pros and cons. Some filters, like the mesh filter, require more maintenance than a baffle filter. It also depends on your cooking environment. Baffle filters are sturdier then mesh filters.

The latest technology in the world of chimneys is the filterless Chimney. The Chimneys do not have any filter but a container where the oil & grease gets accumulated, which needs to be detached and cleaned. You also end up saving repair and replacement costs of the filter and its locks/clips.

What should be the size of the Chimney?

This depends on the size of your cooking area or your hob. How many burners do you have in your cooktop/hobs? The ideal size can be between 60–90cm.

If your Kitchen has 2/3/4 burner cooktop/hobs of 60 cm width, then a 60 cm or 75 cm width chimney is fine.

If you have 3/4/5 burner cooktop/hobs of width 61–75 cm, then go with a 75/90cm width chimney.

If you have 3/4/5 burner cooktop/hobs with a 76–90 cm width, then opt for a chimney with a width of 90 cm.

It is the width of a cooktop/hob that is to be considered and not the number of burners.

It is always recommended to install a chimney that is 3–6 inches wider than the cooktop/hob for the Chimney to work efficiently.

What should be the suction power of the motor?

It depends on various factors like the size of the Kitchen, the length of the ducting, the number of bends in the duct, and cooking habits.

If the length of ducting is up to 7ft with 1–2 bends, then a chimney with a suction power of at least 1000m^3 is required.

If the length of ducting is between 8–14ft, with 1–3 bends, then a chimney with a suction power of at least 1200m^3 is required.

If the length of ducting is 15ft and above, with 1–4 bends, then a chimney with a suction power of at least $1400m^3$ is required.

Can I get a chimney that makes less noise?

You can use different speed level settings to reduce the level of noise. On average, a chimney has 9 speed levels. When you cook something that does not produce lots of smell and smoke, you can run your Chimney at a speed of 1/2/3 for ventilation. This will produce negligible sound. When the smoke and the smell are stronger, you can increase the speed to 8/9.

Opt for a chimney with a brushless D.C. motor. It is not entirely noiseless, but it definitely produces less noise compared to other models.

If your budget is high, you can opt for a Split chimney, which works like a Split Air conditioner.

What should be the distance between the Chimney and the cooking area?

The Chimney should be installed at a height of 30–32 inches from the cooktop/hobs.

How should cleaning & maintenance be done?

Someone from an authorized service centre must clean the inner body and the motor twice a year. You can clean the mesh filter once a week by yourself. In the case of a baffle filter, you need to clean it once a fortnight. Some chimneys come equipped with an auto-cleaning mechanism–the heat melts the oil and grease deposits, which get accumulated in a container. Nonetheless, it would be best to get a technician once a year to clean the Chimney properly.

A Bonus Tip

In case you have an Interior Designer/Architect/Modular Kitchen vendor/Contractor/builder designing/executing your kitchen renovation, please do remember to communicate with them how many burners in a cooktop you use in your Kitchen.

Based on the number of burners, you need to select a cooktop of the size that suits your Kitchen. After you have selected the Cooktop, you need to select a chimney for your Kitchen before renovating the Kitchen.

I have come across many customers who have either failed to discuss it with their professional who is executing the work and felt that the Chimney & Cooktop is to be selected once the renovation is complete, due to which the space left for the installation of the Chimney is insufficient. I will explain this with a case study.

A customer named Ms.Agarwal (name changed for privacy reasons) came to my showroom to select a chimney & Cooktop after her Kitchen was completely renovated by her interior designer.

Ms. Agarwal always cooked in a 3 burner cooktop and will be comfortable using a 3 burner cooktop in the future too. The width of a 3 burner cooktop varies between 70–90 cm depending on the model.

Since the size of the Kitchen was small, the space allocated for the Chimney was sufficient to accommodate only a 60 cm width chimney.

Now with limited space for a 60 cm chimney, she had options to select from, either a 2/4 burner cooktop with 60 cm width. With a very heavy heart, she had to compromise with a 3 burner cooktop.

I could empathize with how difficult it is for a homemaker to let go of something they are comfortable using in their day-to-day life.

Had Ms. Agarwal discussed the same with her Interior Designer and selected a chimney & cooktop/hobs before her Kitchen renovation began, this situation could have been eliminated.

This is just 1 real-life example I have shared with you. In my day-to-day life, I come across many such cases where the customer wanted to install a chimney/hob of their choice, but they regret their decision to select one after renovation work is complete.

If you don't want to come across a situation like Ms. Agarwal and other such customers, always remember to select a chimney & cooktop/hob at the time of planning your renovation work with your Interior Designer/Architect/Modular Kitchen vendor/ Contractor/Builder.

Let's keep talking…

My Invitation To You

My objective is that this book should not be the end of our conversation but the initiation of a long term association.

I urge you to reach out to me for anything you would like to discuss about these "MODERN GADGETS" –**Chimneys & Built-in Hobs.**

Email: talkto@gurjotsinghgulati.com

Contact: 9830184464

www.ingramcontent.com/pod-product-compliance
Ingram Content Group UK Ltd.
Pitfield, Milton Keynes, MK11 3LW, UK
UKHW021654190726
13853UKWH00001B/258